FERRARI

By Jennifer Colby

45TH PARALLEL PRESS

Published in the United States of America by Cherry Lake Publishing Group
Ann Arbor, Michigan
www.cherrylakepublishing.com

Reading Adviser: Beth Walker Gambro, MS Ed., Reading Consultant, Yorkville, IL
Book Designer: Jen Wahi

Photo Credits: © Lawrence Carmichael/Shutterstock, cover, 1; © Realy Easy Star/Toni Spagone/Alamy Stock Photo, 4; © Dmitry Eagle Orlov/Shutterstock, 6, 7; © Konstantin Egorychev/Shutterstock, 8; © Holapaco77/Wikimedia, 10; © MARKA/Alamy Stock Photo, 11; © Lukas Raich/Wikimedia, 11; © Oleksandr Grechin/Shutterstock, 13; © Mau47/Shutterstock, 14; Archive PL/Alamy Stock Photo, 16; © Hafiz Johari/Shutterstock, 17; © Jarlat Maletych/Shutterstock, 18, 19, 24; © Giftzwerg88/Wikimedia, 20; © ddimcars/Alamy Stock Photo, 21; © Johnnie Rik/Shutterstock, 22; © Artoholics/Shutterstock, 23; © Sunshine Seeds/Shutterstock, 26; © cla78/Shutterstock, 27; © Toby Parsons/Shutterstock, 29; © IanDagnall Computing/Alamy Stock Photo, 30; © Mike Mareen/Shutterstock, 31; © oksana.perkins/Shutterstock, 31.

45th Parallel Press is an imprint of Cherry Lake Publishing Group.

Library of Congress Cataloging-in-Publication Data

Names: Colby, Jennifer, 1971- author.
Title: Ferrari / by Jennifer Colby.
Description: Ann Arbor, Michigan: Cherry Lake Publishing, [2022] | Series:
  Floored! Supercars
Identifiers: LCCN 2022005394 | ISBN 9781668909546 (hardcover) | ISBN
  9781668911143 (paperback) | ISBN 9781668912737 (ebook) | ISBN
  9781668914328 (pdf)
Subjects: LCSH: Ferrari automobile--Juvenile literature. | Sports
  cars--Juvenile literature.
Classification: LCC TL215.F47 C638 2022 | DDC 629.222/2--dc23/eng/20220210
LC record available at https://lccn.loc.gov/2022005394

Printed in the United States of America by
Corporate Graphics

ABOUT THE AUTHOR:

Jennifer Colby is a school librarian in Ann Arbor, Michigan. She does not drive a supercar, but she likes going to auto shows to see what they look like.

Table of Contents

One place to see a Ferrari supercar is at an auto show.

CHAPTER 1

What Are Supercars?

Cars get us where we need to go. We drive them to school and work. We drive them to the grocery store or a friend's house. If we need to go someplace, a car can get us there. But some car owners want a car that is more than a way to get from place to place. They want a car that is known for its high **performance**, **luxury**, or **technological** features. Performance is how well something works. Luxury means great comfort. Technological means using science and engineering. These car owners want to drive a **supercar**.

A supercar is a sports car. It is designed to provide a high-level driving experience. Drivers of supercars expect excellent **acceleration**, **handling**, and **maneuvering**. Acceleration is the act of moving faster. Handling is the way a car moves when it is driven. Maneuvering is a skillful way of moving.

Supercars are also known for their unique looks. You might see one of these eye-catching cars and admire it.

Have you seen a Ferrari driving down the road? If so, then you have seen a supercar! What makes these cars so special?

Let's find out more about Ferraris.

Ferrari is known for its signature red color.

Enzo Ferrari first used this logo on his cars in 1947.

CHAPTER 2

Ferrari History

The carmaker Ferrari was founded by Italian race car driver Enzo Ferrari. Born in 1898, Ferrari began racing cars in 1920. Ferrari won his first **Grand Prix** in 1923. Grand Prix races are held throughout Europe. They are run on closed roads or on courses designed to be like real-life roadways. Ferrari retired from racing with 11 Grand Prix wins. In 1939, he decided to focus on making fast cars of his own. He opened a factory in Modena, Italy.

Ferrari's logo includes a horse on a yellow background. The top of the logo includes the colors of the Italian flag—green, white, and red. Ferrari created the logo in memory of a famous World War II (1939–1945) Italian pilot. The pilot had the horse image painted on the side of his plane.

The Ferrari logo was used in 1947 on the Ferrari 125 Sport. It was the first Ferrari model to race in the Grand Prix circuit. It won the Rome Grand Prix in 1947. Only 2 Ferrari 125 Sports were ever made!

Ferrari once said, "If you see what a competitor is doing and it is better than what you are doing, you have to surpass them to ensure your car is better."

Ferrari's race cars soon became almost unbeatable. Ferrari is the only racing team to compete in every Formula 1 racing season since 1950. Formula 1 is the highest level of international auto racing competitions in the Grand Prix racing circuit. Formula 1 cars are the fastest racing cars in the world. Ferrari cars rule Formula 1 racing with a total of 238 wins. The Ferrari racing team holds nearly every Formula 1 record.

Ferrari headquarters in Maranello, Italy.

Enzo Ferrari (left) in his workshop.

Race car driver
Maya Weug.

Maya Weug at a
Formula 4 race.

Behind the Wheel

Maya Weug was born in 2004. She started racing go-karts in Spain at age 7. In 2020, she joined the "Girls on Track Rising Stars" program. Out of 20 young women competing, Maya was picked as the best. As the winner, Maya joined the Ferrari Driver Academy. She is the first female driver to do so.

The academy's goal is to encourage and train young Ferrari drivers. At the academy, Maya learns all aspects of race car driving. Besides on-the-track training, she studies the rules and history of the sport. Many academy students have gone on to race at the Formula 1 level.

The 166 Inter was Ferrari's first grand touring car.

CHAPTER 3
Ferrari Evolution

Since the company's beginning, Ferrari's goal has been to make high-performance race cars. But the company also makes road cars. The 166 Inter was based on a model that was very successful on the race course. It was Ferrari's first **grand touring** car. A grand touring car is designed for high speeds and long-distance drives. Only 38 models of the 166 Inter were made.

Up until the 1960s, Ferrari's road cars were designed with the engine in the front. That changed in 1968 with the Ferrari Dino. The Ferrari Dino was named after Enzo Ferrari's son. Alfredo "Dino" Ferrari worked for the company as an **engineer**. An engineer is a person with scientific training who designs and builds things.

Dino was designing a new engine when he died from a severe type of **muscular dystrophy**. Muscular dystrophy is a disease that causes weakness of the muscles. The "Dino" logo on the car was based on Dino Ferrari's own signature.

It was the first Ferrari with a **mid-engine layout**. A mid-engine layout puts the car's engine in front of the rear-wheel **axles** but behind the front axle. Axles are the metal rods that connect the wheels on either side of the car. This layout is now the standard for supercar designs.

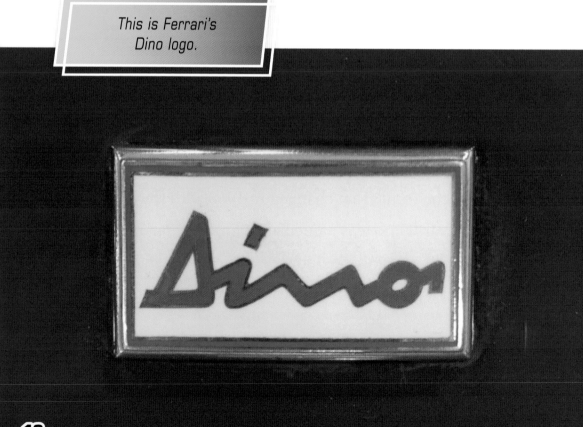

This is Ferrari's Dino logo.

A Ferrari on a Formula 1 race course.

In 1984, Ferrari introduced the Testarossa. *Testa rossa* means "red head" in Italian. The design of the Testarossa was a big change for Ferrari. Previous Ferrari models were known for their smooth, curvy lines. The Testarossa had more straight lines in its design.

It was made famous in television shows and video games of the time. Almost 10,000 Testarossa cars were produced from 1984 through 1996. It is one of the most popular Ferrari models of all time.

The Testarossa is an iconic Ferrari design.

In 2019, Ferrari introduced the SF90 Stradale. It was Ferrari's first **hybrid** car. A hybrid car is powered with a gasoline engine and an electric motor. The Stradale design includes 3 electric motors and an **internal combustion engine**. An internal combustion engine uses gasoline to power the engine that runs the car.

The Stradale is fast! It can go from 0 to 60 miles (97 kilometers) per hour in 2 seconds. That makes it one of the fastest cars on the road today. It would take an average car more than 8 seconds to do what the Ferrari can do.

A rear view of the Ferrari SF90 Stradale.

The Ferrari SF90 Stradale.

Ferrari's most popular paint color is Rosso Corsa. This means "racing red."

Fast Facts

RACING LEGENDS

- Production of the first Ferrari race car was delayed because of World War II.

- Ferrari drivers have won more than 5,000 professional races.

- The most successful Ferrari driver is Michael Schumacher. He won 48 Grand Prix races from 2000 to 2004.

- Maya Weug is the first female driver to be a member of the Ferrari Driver Academy.

- Ferrari makes race cars for other racing teams around the world.

- Ferrari is the oldest and most successful Formula 1 racing team.

Which Ferrari is your favorite?

CHAPTER 4
Ferrari Today

Every Ferrari is unique. Each owner can choose exactly how their car looks. The company's Tailor-Made program allows the buyer to select specific interior looks, accessories, colors, and even tire **tread**! A tread is the pattern of raised lines on the part of a tire that touches the ground.

In 2022, Ferrari will introduce its first **SUV**, the Purosangue. SUV stands for sport utility vehicle. An SUV is a car designed to be used on rough surfaces but is often used on city roads. In the past, Ferrari was reluctant to make an SUV. The company preferred to focus on sports and race cars.

Ferraris are not cheap! The least expensive model is the Portofino. It costs $215,000. The most expensive road car in production is the Ferrari SF90 Stradale. It costs $507,000. The Monza SP1 is a one-seater. It is not even legal to drive on roads in the United States. It costs around $1.8 million.

The expense of owning a Ferrari does not stop at purchase. It costs a lot of money to maintain a Ferrari.

A worker carefully cleans the surface of a Ferrari.

Ferrari sales went down in 2020 and increased in 2021.

Cost of Ownership

MODEL	PRICE
2021 Honda CRV	$25,350
2021 Ford Escape	$25,555
2021 Chevy Suburban	$52,300

MODEL	PRICE
2021 Ferrari Portofino	$215,000
2021 Ferrari Roma	$222,630
2021 Ferrari F8 Spider	$274,000
2021 Ferrari 812 Superfast	$350,000
2021 Ferrari SF90 Stradale	$507,000
2021 Ferrari Monza SP1	$1,800,000

No matter how much it is driven, a Ferrari requires annual service. This can cost up to $7,000! A Ferrari engine needs work every 3 to 5 years. That will cost a Ferrari owner about $30,000. One reason it costs so much to maintain a Ferrari is because the parts are so expensive. One bolt for a Ferrari could cost more than $45. A bolt for a normal car costs only about $5. Car buyers must decide if they can afford the expense of a Ferrari.

The 812 Superfast is a popular Ferrari model.

Timeline of a Legend

■ Enzo Ferrari starts his own car company in Modena, Italy

1939

■ 125 Sport is produced and wins a Grand Prix race

1947

1950

1943

■ Ferrari participates in the first Formula 1 championship race

■ Ferrari factory moves to Maranello, Italy

1898

■ Enzo Ferrari is born in Italy

- Testarossa is
  produced

1984

- SF90 Stradale hybrid
  car is produced

2019

2002

- Enzo is produced

1968

- Dino is produced

Find Out More

BOOKS

Mason, Paul. *Italian Supercars: Ferrari, Lamborghini, Maserati*. New York, NY: PowerKids Press, 2018.

Smith, Ryan. *Ferrari*. New York, NY: AV2, 2021.

WEBSITES

Ferrari—History
https://www.ferrari.com/en-EN/history

Kiddle—Ferrari Facts for Kids
https://kids.kiddle.co/Ferrari

Glossary

acceleration (ik-seh-luh-RAY-shuhn) the act of moving faster

axles (AK-suhlz) the metal rods that connect the wheels on either side of the car

engineer (en-juh-NEER) person with scientific training who designs and builds complicated products

Grand Prix (GRAND PREE) European car race run on closed roads or on courses designed to be like real-life roadways

grand touring (GRAND TOOR-ing) designed for high speeds and long-distance drives

handling (HAND-ling) the way a car moves when it is driven

hybrid (HYE-bruhd) powered with a gasoline engine and an electric motor

internal combustion engine (in-TUHR-nuhl kuhm-BUHS-chuhn EN-juhn) an engine powered by gasoline or other fuel

luxury (LUHK-shuh-ree) great comfort and wealth

maneuvering (muh-NOO-vuh-ring) moving in a skillful way

mid-engine layout (mihd-EN-juhn LAY-owt) when the engine is in front of the rear-wheel axles and behind the front axle

muscular dystrophy (MUH-skyuh-luhr DIH-struh-fee) disease that causes increasing weakness of the muscles

performance (puh-FOHR-muhns) how well something functions or works

supercar (SOO-puhr-kar) sports car designed for a high-level driving experience

SUV (ESS YOO VEE) vehicle designed to be used on rough surfaces but often used on city roads

technological (tek-nuh-LAH-jih-kuhl) relating to science and engineering

tread (TREHD) pattern of raised lines on the part of a tire that touches the ground

Index